WITHDRAWN

AMERICA'S ARMED FORCES

The U.S. AIR FORCE

DAVID JORDAN

WORLD ALMANAC® LIBRARY

Please visit our web site at: www.worldalmanaclibrary.com
For a free color catalog describing World Almanac® Library's list of high-quality books
and multimedia programs, call 1-800-848-2928 (USA) or 1-800-387-3178 (Canada).
World Almanac® Library's fax: (414) 332-3567.

Library of Congress Cataloging-in-Publication Data

Jordan, David.
   The U.S. Air Force / by David Jordan.
      p. cm. — (America's armed forces)
   Includes bibliographical references and index.
   ISBN 0-8368-5679-1 (lib. bdg.)
   ISBN 0-8368-5686-4 (softcover)
   1. United States. Air Force—Juvenile literature.   2. United States. Air Force—Vocational
guidance—Juvenile literature.   I. Title: United States Air Force.   II. Title.   III. Series.
UG633.J67   2004
358.4'00973—dc22   2004042790

First published in 2005 by
World Almanac® Library
330 West Olive Street, Suite 100
Milwaukee, WI 53212 USA

Developed by Amber Books Ltd.
Editor: James Bennett
Designer: Colin Hawes
Photo research: Sandra Assersohn, Natasha Jones
World Almanac® Library editor: Mark Sachner
World Almanac® Library art direction: Tammy West
World Almanac® Library production: Jessica Morris

Picture Acknowledgements
U.S. DoD/U.S. Air Force: cover, 4, 5, 11, 16, 18, 20, 22, 25, 27, 29, 30, 31, 32, 33, 35, 36, 38,
42 (both); TRH: 6, 7, 8 (U.S. Army), 9, 10, 12, 13, 14, 15, 17t, 19, 21, 24, 26, 28, 39b, 40;
Corbis: 17b; Maps: Patrick Mulrey.

Printed in Canada

1 2 3 4 5 6 7 8 9 08 07 06 05 04

About the Author

DAVID JORDAN is a lecturer at the Joint Services Command and Staff College in
Wiltshire, England, where he teaches Intermediate and Advanced Staff courses. He has
held posts at the Universities of Birmingham, Worcester, and Keele and has a Ph.D.
from the University of Birmingham. He is the author of several books, including
Aircraft Carriers and *The U.S. Navy Seals,* and currently lives in Oxfordshire, England.

Table of Contents

Introduction

Right: A modern-day A-10 Thunderbolt II attack aircraft leads two World War II veterans: a Lockheed P-38 Lightning (center) and a North American P-51 Mustang (rear).

The United States is the most powerfully armed nation in the world today. The U.S. Air Force (USAF) has more combat aircraft than any other country's air force, and these include some of the most technically advanced machines in the world, including the F-117 Nighthawk and B-2 Spirit "stealth" aircraft, designs that are almost invisible to enemy radar. To operate these aircraft, the USAF has over 350,000 personnel around the world. The Air Force is also supported by the Air National Guard (ANG) and the Air Force Reserve (AFRES), made up of part-time personnel who combine their duties with civilian jobs.

Although the United States was among the first nations to see its armed forces take to the air in the late 1900s, the U.S. Air Force was not created until 1947. Until this date, the nation's combat aircraft were divided between the U.S. Navy and the U.S. Army. To properly understand the USAF, it is necessary to look at the full history of the use of air power in the United States, and it is important to remember that the USAF could not operate with pilots and aircrew alone. The people who maintain aircraft and aircraft bases are also invaluable to the USAF.

Since its creation, the U.S. Air Force has seen a great deal of action. It has fought in conflicts in Korea, Vietnam, the former Yugoslavia, Afghanistan, and Iraq. The USAF also maintained part of the United States' nuclear **deterrent** during the Cold War, when the U.S. and its Western European allies were in political conflict with the Soviet Union as a result of the different political systems that existed between the two power **blocs**.

Always on the cutting edge of advances in high technology and training, the USAF will undoubtedly solidify its key position in the defense of the United States against any threats it might face in the future.

Below: A weapons technician prepares an AIM-120 Advanced Medium Range Air-to-Air Missile (AMRAAM) before flight. The missile is beneath the wing of an F-16C fighter/attack aircraft.

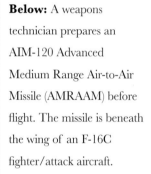

Right: Balloons were used in the Civil War to help Union Army commanders work out where the enemy's troops were located, and to help guide fire from artillery.

The history of the U.S. Air Force actually predates the invention of the airplane. The first use of an aircraft came in the Civil War (1861–1865), when Union forces used balloons to help direct **artillery** fire and observe Confederate positions. Unfortunately, many senior Union officers were unconvinced that balloons were of much use, and by June 1863 the Union forces had stopped using them. The balloonists were part of the Army Signal Corps, which came into being in June 1860. Its purpose was to serve as a visual signaling system for troops, and later, as a telegraph communications system.

Despite the short-lived use of balloons during the Civil War, there were people who recognized that putting an observer in the air to spot enemy positions was a good idea. As a result, the idea of using balloons did not die out. When the United States went to war with Spain in 1898 on the side of Cuba, who wanted independence from Spain, the Army again adopted the notion of using an observer in a balloon. Brigadier-General Adolphus W. Greely, head of the Army Signal Corps, ordered that a balloon should go to Cuba. Unfortunately, the balloon was soon damaged by rifle fire from Spanish troops.

In 1902, the Signal Corps again started to make use of balloons in training, and shortly afterward investigated the use of a dirigible (a balloon with an engine and controls that allow it to be steered by the pilot). Although the experiment was moderately successful, the invention of the airplane in 1903 put an end to early balloon experiments.

Above: Orville (left) and Wilbur Wright were the first to achieve sustained flight in a heavier-than-air powered aircraft.

Early Aircraft

The airplane offered the Army a new means of putting soldiers in the air, but there was doubt at first as to whether the new invention would be of any use. The inventors of the first successful heavier-than-air aircraft, Orville and Wilbur Wright, spent four years trying to convince the War Department that airplanes would be useful for military purposes. The War Department put the Signal Corps in charge of aircraft trials, which began in August 1908, with the brothers teaching Army officers to fly in an aircraft similar to their original 1903 *Flyer*. This process was delayed on September 17, 1908, when the aircraft crashed. The officer under instruction, Lieutenant Thomas E. Selfridge, was killed, becoming the first American military air-crash victim, and Orville Wright, who had been instructing Selfridge, was badly injured. After the Wrights had rebuilt their aircraft, the tests resumed. Overall, the Signal Corps was happy with the results of the trials and bought three more Wright aircraft, as well as two from the Glenn Curtiss Company.

By 1912, the Army had devised a number of tests that prospective pilots had to pass before becoming military aviators. There was still some doubt about the future of aircraft in Army service, but Congress soon passed a bill that made the

aviation section of the Signal Corps a permanent organization, providing funding for additional soldiers.

The Mexican Revolution

The first test for the newly formed Aviation Section of the Signal Corps occurred during the Mexican Revolution (1910–1920). What initially began as a movement to overthrow a **dictatorship** in Mexico grew into a widespread rebellion, with several different groups fighting for power. In late 1915, U.S. president Woodrow Wilson recognized one of the groups as the legitimate Mexican government. In retaliation, one of the other leaders, Pancho Villa, executed some U.S. citizens and then sent his forces to raid the town of Columbus, New Mexico. President Wilson sent the Army to carry out operations against Villa. The air service sent aircraft along, but found that it was difficult to

Above: A Wright Flyer airplane. Although this was the first type tested by the U.S. Army, the pace of aircraft development was so rapid that the Wright brothers' design was soon replaced in service by other more capable types.

Above: A Curtiss JN-3 pictured during the 1916 Mexico Expedition by the U.S. Army. Despite poor weather conditions, the airplanes showed great potential for future use.

carry out flights in the terrible weather over Mexico at that time. Despite this, the pilots learned a lot about flying in awkward conditions and how they might best use their airplane to assist the troops on the ground. They returned to the United States in August 1916, but soon found themselves preparing to travel to Europe.

World War I

On April 6, 1917, the United States declared war on Germany and joined the British and French and their allies as they fought to bring World War I (then known as the Great War) to an end. When the aviation section went to fight in France, it was hard to believe that the United States had once led the world in aircraft design. The British, French, and Germans had made great progress, while U.S. military aviation was lagging behind. There were no U.S.-built aircraft suitable for use in France, and U.S. airmen had to make use of British and French-built aircraft. Valuable lessons were learned, however, and the American pilots did well.

One of the senior officers sent to France was Colonel William Mitchell, who was important in the development of U.S. air power. At the time, aircraft were used to support soldiers on the ground, but Mitchell argued that aircraft could

Edward V. Rickenbacker

"Eddie" Rickenbacker drove racing cars before the war, but joined the U.S. air service once the United States entered World War I. He arrived in France in April 1918 with the 94th Aero Squadron, and went on to shoot down 26 German aircraft, making him the most successful American fighter pilot of World War I.

Left: Captain Edward Vernon Rickenbacker, the U.S. "Ace of Aces" in World War I. He is pictured sitting in the cockpit of his SPAD fighter plane.

be used in several important ways. He suggested that they could destroy enemy aircraft while they were on the ground at their bases, thus preventing the enemy from attacking friendly troops. Mitchell also wanted to use aircraft to attack targets well behind the front lines, believing that they could bomb enemy supply lines and factories making enemy military equipment.

World War I ended on November 11, 1918, before Mitchell had an opportunity to demonstrate his ideas. He continued, however, to argue in favor of air operations independent of the Army. Unfortunately, Mitchell expressed his ideas very forcibly, which did not make him popular, particularly when he began to argue that airplanes were much cheaper to build than battleships. When he was given the opportunity to carry out trial bombing attacks against surrendered German battleships, to the Navy's annoyance, Mitchell's aircraft sank three of them, as well as the obsolete U.S. battleship *Alabama*.

The Army and Navy, however, still did not adopt Mitchell's ideas, and he became critical of the two services. This was a breach of military discipline, and

Below: Colonel William "Billy" Mitchell stands alongside a U.S. Army air service fighter airplane.

Above: The captured German battleship *Ostfriesland* was bombed by air service aircraft as part of trials organized by Colonel Mitchell to show how airplanes might be used against ships in a future war.

in 1925, Mitchell was **court-martialed** and resigned from the service.

Eventually, Mitchell's ideas were adopted by other senior air service officers, who became convinced that much of what Mitchell said was correct. Sixteen years after Mitchell's court-martial, Japan attacked the naval base at Pearl Harbor, and the air service was given the opportunity to put some of Mitchell's ideas into practice.

The Lafayette Escadrille

The Lafayette Escadrille was a unit made up of U.S. aviators serving as part of the French air arm during World War I. The airmen had volunteered to fight alongside the French in 1916, before the United States entered the war. They learned a great deal about military air operations, and were the only U.S. airmen to see combat until 1918. Many of the members of the Escadrille went on to command American aviation units.

Right: A member of the crew of a B-17 Flying Fortress shows the clothing and equipment needed to stay alive in the cold temperatures found at the heights at which his aircraft flew.

William Mitchell might have been the most vocal, but he was not the only one thinking about how aircraft might best be used. Other officers continued to develop tactics and strategy for the use of aircraft, and their efforts were recognized in 1926, when Congress passed the Air Corps Act. This increased the importance of the air service (by now called the U.S. Army Air Corps, or USAAC), giving it more funding and representation on the General Staff (the body that ran the Army). These developments meant that it was possible to begin building a much larger air arm. In 1930, the Air Corps issued a requirement for a modern bomber, which resulted in the Martin B-10, an airplane that was faster than most fighters, or pursuit aircraft as they were then known. The following year, the Air Corps was given responsibility for defending the nation's coastlines, a task that was independent of ground forces. This was the first step toward a truly independent air force.

World War II in Europe

Once it was clear that the United States was in danger of being dragged into the war in Europe, President Franklin D. Roosevelt asked Congress to increase defense spending as a precautionary measure. Congress granted his request. Roosevelt returned to Congress for more funds in 1939 and in 1940; once again, Congress agreed. The Air Corps was expanded and placed orders for a whole series of aircraft, including the B-24 Liberator bomber; the B-25 Mitchell and B-26 Marauder medium bombers; and the P-38 Lightning, P-39 Airacobra, and P-40 Warhawk fighter aircraft. The Air Corps also expanded its training program so that there would be more pilots, aircrew, and mechanics to operate the new planes.

On December 7, 1941, Japanese aircraft attacked Pearl Harbor, and the United States declared war against Japan. Two days later, Germany declared war on the United States. By this time, the Air Corps had been expanded further and was renamed the U.S. Army Air Forces

Below: Ground crew prepare bombs for loading into a Martin B-10 bomber. Although the B-10 looks old-fashioned now, it was an advanced aircraft for its day.

(USAAF). The first major act by the USAAF came in April 1942, when B-25 Mitchell bombers were flown from the deck of the aircraft carrier USS *Hornet* to bomb Japan. The raid did not cause major damage, but deeply concerned the Japanese. Although this raid targeted Japan, President Roosevelt knew that forces also had to be sent to Germany. The USAAF was involved in the bombing of many targets important to the German war effort, but these operations were not without cost. The problem facing the USAAF's crews was the opposition posed by German fighter aircraft. The Air Force had thought that the heavy firepower carried by B-17s and B-24s would enable them to fight their way through fighter opposition, both to and from their target, as long as the crews kept in a formation known as a "combat box," meaning that the guns of each aircraft protected not only that airplane, but the ones next to it as well. Unfortunately, this reasoning proved incorrect, and the bombers suffered heavy losses. The problem was solved by the development of escort fighters, such as the P-47 Thunderbolt, the P-38 Lightning, and, the most famous of them all, the P-51 Mustang, which could protect the bombers all the way to Germany and back.

The Air Force was also successful in supporting land operations after June 6, 1944, known as D-Day, when Allied troops invaded France to begin the recapture of lands conquered by Adolf Hitler's troops in 1939 and 1940. To assist the troops on the

Below: A B-25 bomber leaves the deck of the USS *Hornet* to take part in a daring raid on Tokyo. This was the only means of striking back at the Japanese in the first months after the attack on Pearl Harbor.

Left: A B-17 bomber crew. Thousands of U.S. pilots and crew operated from bases in Britain, carrying out dangerous daylight bombing raids.

General Henry Harley Arnold

"Hap" Arnold was born on June 25, 1886, and graduated from West Point in 1907. After service as an infantryman, he was assigned to the Army Signal Corps' air division; during a posting as an instructor, he set a world altitude record. When World War I began, he was sent to Washington, D.C. and worked as a staff officer. Arnold was promoted steadily during the interwar years, and became assistant chief of the USAAC in 1936. He took command of the Air Corps two years later, and then became chief of the USAAF when it was created. Arnold led the USAAF throughout World War II, before handing over command in 1946. Arnold died on January 15, 1950.

General Carl Arthur Spaatz

Carl Spaatz was born in 1891, and joined the Army in 1914 as an infantry officer. He moved to the air service in 1915, and took part in the 1916 expedition to Mexico against Pancho Villa's forces. When the United States entered World War I, Spaatz went to France as commander of the 31st Aero Squadron. He was then posted to instructing duties (again in France) before he joined the 2nd Pursuit Squadron in August 1918. In the remaining two months of the war, he shot down three German aircraft and was awarded the Distinguished Service Cross.

During the 1920s and 1930s, Spaatz served in a variety of Air Force roles, and established an endurance record in 1929, flying an airplane for 150 hours, 50 minutes through the use of air refueling. He was posted to Britain as a military observer in 1939, before returning to Washington, D.C. as chief of USAAF Combat Command. Spaatz returned to the European theater, commanding the Eighth and Twelfth Air Forces; after the invasion of Italy, he became deputy commander of Allied Air Forces in the Mediterranean. In January 1944, Spaatz took command of all bombing operations against Germany, and then moved to a similar position in the Pacific. He succeeded "Hap" Arnold as commanding general of the USAAF, and was the first Air Force chief of staff when the USAF was created. He retired in 1948, and pursued a career with *Newsweek* magazine. Carl Spaatz died on July 14, 1974.

ground, the Air Force flew what are known as "close air support" missions. These involved attacking enemy positions that were stopping Allied troops from advancing. Together with the British Royal Air Force, the USAAF flew numerous missions of this sort, proving quite effective.

War in the Pacific

In the Pacific, the Air Force was equally successful. Air Force fighters shot down many Japanese aircraft and supported troops on the ground by dropping

bombs and firing rockets against Japanese
positions. The Air Force's main contribution,
however, was bombing Japan itself. The Air
Force used a large bomber airplane, the B-29
Stratofortress, to carry out these operations. B-29s
dropped vast numbers of bombs on Japanese
targets, reducing the enemy's ability to fight by
destroying factories that produced war materials
and the transportation systems that carried these
materials to the front line.

In 1945, President Harry Truman decided that
he would try to force the Japanese to surrender
by using a new weapon—the atomic bomb. The
atomic bomb had terrible destructive power, and
it was hoped that dropping one on a Japanese city
would convince the enemy to surrender. On
August 6, 1945, an atomic bomb was dropped
on the city of Hiroshima. The Japanese were
appalled by the human and physical destruction,
but still did not surrender. As a result, a second
atomic bomb was dropped on the city of Nagasaki
on August 9. The Japanese surrendered five days
later. Although the atomic bombs brought the war
to an end, they caused terrible damage. About 100,000 people were killed
or injured in the two bombings, and many people later died as a result of
radiation sickness from the bomb. These heavy casualties caused nuclear
weapons to become controversial, with many people arguing that they were
so terrible they ought to be banned.

With the end of the war, the size of the USAAF was reduced dramatically,
but the apparent threat presented by the Soviet Union meant that the United
States' armed forces would soon increase in size. As they did so, they would
include a totally new armed service—the U.S. Air Force, now independent of
Army control. The Air Force would begin to exploit new technologies right
away, swiftly becoming the most potent air arm the world had ever seen.

Above: Without the
ground crew to service,
prepare, and repair its
aircraft, the Air Force
could not do its job. These
engineers are pictured
preparing a B-17 Flying
Fortress for a mission
during World War II.

Chapter 3
The U.S. Air Force 1947–2001

Right: A line of North American F-86 Sabres on an airfield in Korea during the 1950s. The F-86 was the only United Nations aircraft that could match the Soviet-built MiG-15 fighter and was vital to the USAF in the Korean War.

After World War II ended, there were some disagreements over the best way to provide the most effective air service. This issue was resolved when Congress passed the National Security Act in 1947. This set up a Department of Defense with three military departments: the Army, Navy, and Air Force. The United States Air Force (USAF) was born at an exciting time in military aviation. The first jet aircraft were just starting to be used toward the end of the war, and in 1950, the Air Force started flying the swept-wing F-86 Sabre, one of the most famous fighter aircraft ever built.

The Cold War

The first major test for the USAF came in 1948. After World War II, Germany was occupied by the United States, Britain, France, and the Soviet Union. The capital, Berlin, was deep in the Soviet zone of occupation. As relations between the powers declined, Soviet leader Joseph Stalin decided to blockade the city to prevent supplies, including food, from entering, in an attempt to isolate the city and force out the occupying Western powers. The Allies responded by launching a massive airlift to Berlin, led by U.S aircraft.

Left: C-47 cargo airplanes at Berlin's Tempelhof airport during the Berlin Airlift in 1948.

The Air Force Academy

With the creation of the USAF in 1947, it was necessary to examine how to train the new service's officers. In 1949, Secretary of Defense James Forrestal appointed a board of military and civilian educators, headed by General Dwight D. Eisenhower, then president of Columbia University. In 1950 it recommended the creation of a new academy and that at least 40 percent of the officers taken into service should be academy graduates.

Congressional authorization for the Air Force Academy was given in 1954, and a site near Colorado Springs was chosen. Construction began in 1955 at the site, while instruction started at the Academy's temporary home at Lowry Air Force Base, Denver. Lieutenant General Hubert R. Harmon was recalled from retirement to become the first superintendent. The Academy moved to Colorado Springs in August 1958. All cadets at the Academy work toward a Bachelor of Science degree alongside their Air Force training. This includes flying lessons and parachute instruction, as well as instruction in ethics and a large range of other subjects.

Right: Air Force Academy graduates celebrate as the USAF demonstration team, the Thunderbirds, fly overhead in their F-16s.

The citizens of Berlin remained supplied throughout the winter of 1948–1949, and in May 1949, the Soviets gave up and lifted the blockade.

Although they lost that battle, the Soviets remained a threat. On September 23, 1949, they exploded their own atomic bomb, raising the possibility that they could attack the United States with nuclear weapons. The Air Force responded by developing a large bomber force and a fleet of fighter aircraft that could intercept Soviet aircraft. This constant struggle between the two nations resulted in what became known as the Cold War (1945–1991). This term was used to describe relations between the Soviet bloc and the United States and its allies, which verged on the brink of war without actual warfare ever occurring.

The Korean War

On June 25, 1950, **communist** North Korea invaded South Korea. The United States made efforts to assist the South, which included USAF aircraft sent to cover the evacuation of U.S. citizens. The presence of the USAF was essential, since the South Korean air force had just 16 aircraft, none of which were combat types. The North Korean air force was not strong, and when it ran into American pilots, it suffered a heavy defeat. While the North's air force might not have been strong, its army was. Outnumbered U.S. and South Korean troops were forced to retreat, covered by Air Force fighter-bombers and attack aircraft. Soon, the United Nations (U.N.) approved the dispatch of a U.N. force made up of troops from a number of countries to help the U.S. Army.

The embattled U.N. forces dug in around the southern port of Pusan and held off the attacking North Koreans. Aircraft provided support, attacking enemy troop positions and supply routes that were bringing in more enemy soldiers and ammunition, as well as bombing targets in North Korea. In September, U.S. troops landed at Inchon, well behind Korean lines, which forced the North Koreans to fight on two fronts. By November 1950, U.N. forces had conquered much of North Korea. The Chinese government, however, feared that the United States would attack China next and sent their forces to fight on the side of North Korea. This enabled communist forces to drive the U.N. forces back into South Korea. The Chinese brought with them

Soviet-designed MiG-15 fighter jets, which proved better than the U.S. F-80s and F-84s. When U.S. forces re-equipped with the more advanced F-86 Sabres, however, the balance changed. On July 27, 1953, the war ended without any side able to claim victory.

The Vietnam War

The next major conflict for the Air Force was the Vietnam War (1959–1975). The Air Force played a key ground attack role in Vietnam, attacking targets in North Vietnam and supporting U.S. forces fighting communist **guerrillas** in the South.

Below: Troops and equipment are loaded onto U.S. Army CV-2B (foreground) and ASAF C-123 (rear) cargo airplanes prior to the start of a major offensive against communist guerrillas in Vietnam.

Race and Gender Issues

Until President Truman introduced legislation in 1948, African Americans and white Americans served in segregated units in the U.S. armed forces. In the USAAF, the most famous case was that of the Tuskegee Airmen, made up entirely of African American pilots and ground crew. The squadron was initially discriminated against, when it was given outdated aircraft, but once it received up-to-date equipment its pilots proved to be among the best in the USAAF.

The ending of segregation enabled African American airmen to achieve high ranks. By the early 1970s, African Americans held a variety of command responsibilities, and several held the rank of general officer.

Women have always played a major role in the Air Force, although they were not allowed to fly until the 1970s and it was rare for them to hold command. Women began to take on flying duties in the late 1970s, and it soon became common to see them as pilots and aircrew aboard transport and tanker aircraft. Women, however, were not allowed to serve in combat aircraft until the 1990s. From this period on, women have flown almost every Air Force aircraft type, including B-52 bombers and A-10 tactical aircraft.

Left: The all-female crew of a KC-135 air refueling tanker is photographed after completing a mission over Afghanistan on January 31, 2003. Women now serve aboard almost every type of aircraft in the USAF.

Above: An F-100 Super Sabre fighter bomber is made ready for a ground attack mission in South Vietnam in February 1970.

Although the USAF's aircrews fought bravely, they faced major problems. Political concerns in Washington, D.C. meant that the airmen were not allowed to attack certain targets in North Vietnam, and this made winning the war much more difficult.

Furthermore, the Vietnam War was increasingly unpopular with the American public, and when President Richard Nixon realized that the United States could not win the war, he promised to find a solution to the conflict. He tried negotiating with the North Vietnamese, but the North Vietnamese continued to fight, invading South Vietnam. Nixon ordered massive use of air power, which inflicted huge damage on North Vietnamese combat units and on the facilities in the North used to supply them.

Negotiations resumed, but again the North Vietnamese stalled. Nixon ordered another massive bombing assault in December 1972, and this finally persuaded the North Vietnamese to negotiate seriously. A peace treaty was signed in early 1973, by which time U.S. and allied soldiers had been withdrawn from the country. In 1975 South Vietnam was overrun by the North and the country was unified under a communist government.

After the Vietnam War, the Air Force went back to its Cold War duties, training so that it would be ready for a war with the Soviet Union. By the mid-1980s, the risk of such a war seemed to be lessening as President Ronald Reagan and Soviet president Mikhail Gorbachev began to build better relations between their countries.

The Persian Gulf War (Operation Desert Storm) and Other Conflicts

If the threat from the Soviet Union was reduced, however, that from terrorists and leaders of states hostile to the United States increased. In 1986, a terrorist bomb killed a U.S. soldier in Berlin. There was enough evidence to link this attack to Libya, which had been in dispute with the United States for some years over suspected Libyan support for terrorist groups. In response, President Reagan sent F-111 attack aircraft to bomb key targets in Libya.

By 1990, the Cold War was all but over, but another problem emerged when Iraqi dictator Saddam Hussein invaded Kuwait. The U.N. told Saddam that if he did not withdraw,

Below: The unusual shape of the F-117 Nighthawk is one of the most distinctive in the sky. Designed so that it is almost impossible for enemy radars to detect, the F-117 has been used with great success in operations since Desert Storm in 1991.

Below: The Boeing B-52 entered service in the 1950s as a nuclear bomber, but is now used to carry heavy loads of conventional munitions against major enemy targets.

military action would be taken against him. Saddam ignored this, and on January 17, 1991, a massive, U.S.-led air assault began as part of the campaign to liberate Kuwait, known as Operation Desert Storm. U.S. aircraft dominated the skies over Iraq, using precision-guided bombs to attack vital targets. F-117 Nighthawk "stealth" aircraft, almost invisible to enemy radar, attacked at will, destroying key military installations. B-52s carried out heavy bombing raids against enemy troops in Kuwait, trying to destroy positions that could threaten advancing **coalition** troops. The damage caused to Saddam's forces was so great that the ground war progressed much better than people had thought it would. Kuwait was swiftly liberated, and after 100 hours of fighting, President George H. W. Bush ordered a cease-fire.

After the Gulf War, the 1990s were marked by USAF involvement in conflicts in Europe. The civil war in Yugoslavia was brought to an end in 1995, when U.S. aircraft led raids against Serbian military targets. Then, five years later, the USAF played the lead role in the campaign to prevent Serbian President Slobodan Milosevic from killing ethnic Albanians living in the province of Kosovo. As the twenty-first century began, it was clear that the USAF was likely to be a dominant player in any war that the United States was to fight. No one expected that the next war to confront the country would be started, not by the leader of a state, but by a vicious terrorist group.

Below: General Daniel James, the first African American to hold four-star general rank in the Air Force, is seen here at a press conference in 1973.

Daniel "Chappie" James

Daniel James was born on February 11, 1920. He attended Tuskegee Institute at Tuskegee, Alabama, between 1937 and 1942, earning a degree in physical education. He also completed civilian pilot training and remained at Tuskegee as a civilian instructor pilot in the Army Air Corps Aviation Cadet Program until January 1943, before joining the USAAF in July that year. He saw service in the Philippines during World War II and flew 101 combat missions in Korea between 1950 and 1951. He then flew air defense fighters in the United States until 1960, when he was posted to the 81st Tactical Fighter Wing in England. James flew combat missions in Vietnam between 1966 and 1967 as part of the famed 8th Tactical Fighter Wing. General James was promoted to the rank of four-star general on September 1, 1975, and was the first African American to hold the highest rank in the USAF. He retired from active service on February 1, 1978, but tragically died of a heart attack just three weeks later.

Right: An airman stands guard in front of a C-130 transport in Afghanistan. Aircraft such as the C-130 are vital to the U.S. armed forces, taking personnel and equipment to trouble spots all over the world.

On September 11, 2001, terrorists **hijacked** four airliners, crashing two into the World Trade Center and another into the Pentagon, while the fourth crashed in open country in western Pennsylvania during the struggle that occurred as passengers attempted to retake control of the aircraft. In the aftermath of the horrific attacks, the United States gathered evidence indicating that they had been carried out by members of Osama bin Laden's al-Qaeda organization.

Bin Laden had found safe haven in Afghanistan, which had been in chaos since the Soviet invasion of 1979. When Soviet troops withdrew 10 years later, the different Afghan resistance movements turned on each other. Bin Laden sided with the Taliban movement, which had managed to establish itself as the nation's government. This meant that he was able to establish a firm base for al-Qaeda within Afghanistan. President George W. Bush demanded that the Taliban hand over bin Laden so that he could face trial for the September 11 attacks. When the Afghan **regime** refused, President Bush started military action against both the Taliban and the al-Qaeda forces in the country.

The war in Afghanistan was quite different from most conflicts the United States had engaged in up to that point. Reaching targets by air proved difficult for the USAF, since there were few facilities for aircraft in neighboring countries. Although some bases were made available, many aircraft had to fly long distances, relying on in-flight refueling. Attacking aircraft made use of new

Left: Two crew chiefs examine paperwork as they stand in front of a B-2 Spirit. The B-2 is the most sophisticated bomber in the world, using "stealth" technology to remain almost invisible to enemy radar.

bombs guided to their targets with information obtained from **satellites**, as well as using laser-guided weapons. Al Qaeda and Taliban (AQT) forces had no answer to air power; even the caves in which they hid were vulnerable to well-directed air attacks. U.S. forces combined with local Afghan troops to fight the AQT, and they were able to call upon heavy air support. AQT forces were quickly driven back, and within a matter of weeks, the Taliban had been overthrown and Al Qaeda members forced to flee.

War in Iraq

The global war on terrorism took the USAF to Iraq next. After the 1990–91 Gulf War, Saddam Hussein was allowed to remain in power; however, the USAF patrolled the skies above Iraq, making sure that Saddam didn't launch air attacks against his neighbors. President Bush's concerns about Saddam providing chemical, biological, or even nuclear weapons technology to terrorist groups led to attempts to force Saddam to allow unrestricted inspections and obey U.N. resolutions preventing him from developing or possessing such weapons. These efforts failed, and President Bush, with the backing of Congress, decided that the only means of dealing with Saddam was to use force, despite serious

Right: Well protected against the cold of an English winter, USAF Airman 1st Class Jacqueline Sullivan connects a fuel nozzle to ground equipment at RAF Mildenhall.

disagreements about this within both the United States and the international community. On March 19, 2003, President Bush told Saddam that he should leave Iraq within 48 hours if he wished to avoid war. The next night, two F-117 Nighthawk stealth fighters bombed targets in Baghdad, and it was rumored that they were trying to kill Saddam Hussein. While they did not kill the dictator, who was captured by U.S. ground troops months later, it was quickly apparent that the early air attacks had stopped the Iraqi high command from organizing its forces.

The Air Force carried out several types of missions during the campaign, known as Operation Iraqi Freedom. Some missions involved attacks against targets used to plan Iraqi military operations, while others were carried out in support of advancing U.S. ground forces. Transport aircraft made sure that U.S. troops were supplied properly, and were also used to drop paratroops in northern Iraq. Refueling tankers resupplied attack aircraft with fuel in midair, while other aircraft used their advanced equipment to locate and track the movement of Iraqi forces. The war also saw the use of robot aircraft known as Uninhabited Air Vehicles (UAVs). UAVs were used to find Iraqi ground forces and pass the information on to attack aircraft to allow them to bomb their targets. Major combat operations in Iraq ended on May 1, 2003, although fighting continued on the ground between guerilla forces and occupying coalition troops.

Below: A Predator unmanned aerial vehicle in Iraq. The Predator is used for reconnaissance missions, and can carry Hellfire missiles for use in combat.

Air Force Operations

In any campaign, the Air Force has several tasks. The two most important are controlling the air and carrying out attacks against enemy targets. Control of the air means preventing an enemy from using its air force in anything other than a limited way. There are a number of types of attacks against enemy targets. These are usually divided into two categories: strategic and tactical. Strategic targets are those that have a direct effect on stopping the enemy from fighting as he wishes. This may mean bombing communications centers so that the enemy commanders cannot tell their troops what to do, or it can mean attacking transportation targets, such as bridges and railroad **sidings**. Tactical targets are usually those on or near the battlefield. They can include targets such as troop concentrations or tanks and fighting vehicles.

Although combat operations receive the most attention from writers, it is important to note that other aircraft play a vital role in modern war. To keep friendly forces supplied with fuel, ammunition, and food, transport aircraft are vitally important. Refueling tankers are also essential. They enable aircraft to fly long distances to carry out their missions, resupplying them with fuel when required. This is particularly important for bomber aircraft. Without refueling tankers, these planes would have to land and take on more fuel along the way, making their job far more difficult. The combination of precise weapons and a large air force means that the USAF is the most powerful in the world and able

Guided Weapons

Until the late 1960s, it was difficult to ensure that a bomb would hit its target or even fall near enough to damage it. This lack of accuracy also meant that the risk to civilians nearby was high. To overcome the problem, the U.S. Air Force developed laser-guided bombs and others guided through the use of specialized television technology (known as electro-optically guided bombs). Laser guided bombs are, as their name suggests, guided to their targets by laser. Electro-optical weapons have a large TV seeker at the front, allowing the pilot or weapons system operator in the airplane to see the target on a screen in the cockpit. The TV seeker is then locked on to the target, and the bomb is released.

Left: The damage caused to one of Saddam Hussein's palaces by a 5,000-lb (2,267-kg) precision-guided weapon can be seen clearly in this photograph. The man on the right is a weapons effect specialist, assessing the effectiveness of air attacks on key targets.

to play a decisive part in military operations. U.S. aircraft can rapidly destroy the enemy's capability to wage war, both by attacking command and control centers and troop concentrations. Because so many different targets can be attacked at once, it makes it extremely difficult for an opponent to carry out effective resistance for any length of time.

Chapter 5
USAF Organization and Aircraft

Right: Troops stand in front of a huge C-5 Galaxy transport aircraft. One of the largest aircraft in the world, the Galaxy carries enormous amounts of cargo over intercontinental distances.

To carry out its missions, the USAF employs a large number of aircraft. This chapter looks at a few of the most important ones and at aircraft that will be joining the Air Force in the future. It also explains how the Air Force is organized.

F-15A/C Eagle

The F-15A and C models are single-seat fighter aircraft, and form the primary air combat type of the Air Force. The Eagle was designed in the 1970s, and the first ones entered service in 1975. Despite its age, the Eagle is still regarded as one of the best combat aircraft in the world. It is armed with a multibarrel M61 20mm cannon and can carry up to eight air-to-air missiles. These can be a mix of AIM-7 Sparrow and AIM-120 AMRAAM (advanced medium-range air-to-air missile) radar-guided missiles and AIM-9 Sidewinder infrared-guided missiles.

F-16 Fighting Falcon

In the 1970s, the Air Force realized that it would not be able to afford as many F-15s as it wanted and looked for a smaller, less expensive airplane. The F-16 entered service in 1979 and has undergone a series of modifications to keep it up-to-date. From a fairly basic aircraft, the F-16 has developed into an advanced and effective multirole aircraft. It can carry almost every weapon the U.S. Air Force uses. It is armed with a single M61 multibarrel cannon and has nine **pylons** on which bombs, missiles, and fuel tanks can be stored. The F-16 is one of the most widely exported airplanes in the world today. Although it is officially called the "Fighting Falcon," most of its pilots refer to the type as the "Viper."

Air Force Commands

The headquarters of the USAF is located in Washington, D.C., and is divided into nine commands, each of which reports to the Chief of Staff of the Air Force. In addition to the nine commands, the Air National Guard and the Air Force Academy fit into the chain of command as what are known as Direct Reporting Units. The nine commands are as follows:

Air Combat Command
Air Mobility Command
Air Education and Training Command
Air Force Reserve Command
Air Force Special Operations Command
Air Force Material Command
United States Air Forces Europe
Pacific Air Forces

With the exception of Special Operations Command and Material Command, each command contains numbered air forces, each with a headquarters located at a major base. Each of these air forces contains several formations known as wings. Each wing has an operations group with aircrew, airplane squadrons, and intelligence units, plus maintenance and support groups, which do everything from maintaining the aircraft to providing security forces.

Above: An F-16C strike fighter pictured during a mission over Iraq prior to Operation Iraqi Freedom. The F-16 is currently the mainstay of USAF tactical forces.

B-52 Stratofortress

The B-52 is the most famous bomber aircraft in the world. The first B-52s entered service with the USAF in the mid-1950s, serving in a nuclear attack role. In Vietnam, B-52s were used to attack Viet Cong targets in South Vietnam and then targets in the north. When the Cold War ended, a large number of B-52s were retired from service, but over 80 still remain in active use today. The B-52 has been constantly updated, and has seen action in all the major conflicts undertaken by the United States in recent years. The Air Force intends to carry on using the B-52 until about 2040, when some aircraft will be around 80 years old.

F-117 Nighthawk

The F-117 was the first stealth aircraft to enter service, in 1983, although it was kept secret for several years. The F-117's design ensures that enemy radar stations find it almost impossible to detect, and unlike conventional aircraft, F-117s normally fly missions without close escort. The airplane was used quite

USAF Bases Around the World

This map shows the locations of major USAF bases around the world.

effectively in Operation Desert Storm, and has seen considerable use since. Only one of the type has been shot down despite the fact that it is used to carry out some of the most difficult and dangerous bombing missions.

C-130 Hercules Family

The C-130 is the standard transport plane of the USAF and numerous other air forces. Although it joined the Air Force in

Right: Cockpit checks are carried out in an F-117 Nighthawk prior to a night bombing mission. The Nighthawk, as its name suggests, is almost always used for attacks under the cover of darkness.

the 1950s, nothing better for the job has been designed, and new versions of the same design are still purchased. In addition to transportation, the Hercules is used for special operations missions and electronic warfare. Another version, the AC-130 gunship, is employed for special attack missions, using a variety of guns (including a 105-mm howitzer).

C-17 Globemaster III
The C-17 is the newest transport to be used by the Air Force. It can carry an M1 Abrams Main Battle Tank and can take off and land at primitive airfields near to the front line, ensuring that equipment reaches soldiers quickly. The USAF has 120 Globemasters currently in service.

C-135 Stratotanker
The C-135 is based on the Boeing 707 airliner, and is used in a large number of tasks, each task requiring a slightly different version. For example, the KC-135 is a refueling tanker, while the EC-135 carries out electronic warfare tasks. RC-135s are used to gather intelligence information by intercepting enemy communications.

Right: An M1 Abrams Main Battle Tank is offloaded from a C-17 Globemaster III. The C-17 is the USAF's newest strategic transport, with some 120 in service.

U-2

The U-2 is a high-altitude reconnaissance airplane, used to gather information about enemy installations, either by using powerful cameras or electronic equipment. The first U-2s joined the Air Force in the late 1950s, and some were used to fly over the Soviet Union during the Cold War.

In addition to these aircraft, the USAF has a number of aircraft that, at the time of this writing, are yet to enter full service:

F/A-22 Raptor

The F/A-22 is the most expensive fighter aircraft ever built, largely because of the high levels of technology it employs. It uses a stealth design to make it more difficult for enemy forces to find it and then attack it, and carries its **armament** inside weapons bays in the **fuselage**. It can also cruise at supersonic speeds,

USAF Bases in the United States

This map shows the locations of major Air Force bases across the United States.

McChord • Fairchild • Malmstrom • Minot • Grand Forks

Ellsworth

Mountain Home • Hanscom

Francis E. Warren • Offutt • Wright-Patterson • McGuire

Hill • Whiteman • Bolling • Dover • Andrews

Beale • USAF Academy • Falcon • Scot • Langley

Travis • McClellan • Peterson • McConnell

Nellis • Vance • Tinker • Seymour Johnson

Vandenberg • Edwards • Kirtland • Altus • Arnold • Pope

Los Angeles • Luke • Cannon • Sheppard • Little Rock • Columbus • Shaw

Davis-Monthan • Holloman • Dyess • Robins • Charleston

Maxwell

Goodfellow • Barksdale • Moody

Alaska • Lackland • Keesler • Eglin

Hawaii • Laughlin • Randolph • Hurlburt Field • Tyndall

Eielson • Kelly • Brooks

Elmendorf • Hickam • MacDill • Patrick

Above: An F/A-22 Raptor, the USAF's newest fighter. Developed at enormous cost, the Raptor will be the best air combat aircraft the world has ever seen.

Right: One of the X-35 Joint Strike Fighter test aircraft comes in to land. The developed version of this airplane, the F-35, will replace the F-16 and A-10 in USAF service.

making it difficult to intercept. The F/A-22 can be used for attack missions, carrying up to four JDAM satellite-guided bombs instead of air-to-air missiles. As well as its missile armament, the F/A-22 carries an updated version of the M61 multibarrel 20-mm cannon.

F-35 Joint Strike Fighter

The F-35 is the result of a major development program, and the type will eventually be used by the Air Force, Navy, Marine Corps, and a number of the United States' allies. The Air Force will use the F-35 to replace F-16s and A-10s starting in 2008. The F-35 uses stealth technology like that on the F/A-22, but is designed primarily for attack missions. It carries its armament in internal weapons bays, and will have a single 27-mm cannon in addition to its bombs and missiles.

Table of Ranks

Rank	Grade	Rank	Grade
General of the Air Force (5-Star General)		Chief Master Sergeant of the Air Force	E-9
General (4-Star General)	O-10	Chief Master Sergeant/First Sergeant/	
Lieutenant General (3-Star General)	O-9	Command Chief Master Sergeant	E-9
Major General (2-Star General)	O-8	Senior Master Sergeant/First Sergeant	E-8
Brigadier-General (1-Star General)	O-7	Master Sergeant/First Sergeant	E-7
Colonel	O-6	Technical Sergeant	E-6
Lieutenant-Colonel	O-5	Staff Sergeant	E-5
Major	O-4	Senior Airman	E-4
Captain	O-3	Airman First Class	E-3
First Lieutenant	O-2	Airman	E-2
Second Lieutenant	O-1	Airman Basic	E-1

The rank of General of the Air Force is only awarded in wartime; only General H. H. Arnold has ever held this rank. The name of the rank of noncommissioned officers at grades E-7 to E-9 depends on the nature of their job. They have the same levels of pay and seniority. There is only one Chief Master Sergeant of the Air Force, who is the senior enlisted person in the service.

Time Line

1861	Balloons used for aerial observation work in U.S. Civil War
1903	December 17: Wright brothers make first manned flight
1916	Aircraft used in expedition against Pancho Villas' forces in Mexico
1918	July/August: United States Air Service (USAS) carries out bombing operations in France; November 11: World War I ends
1926	USAS is renamed U.S. Army Air Corps (USAAC)
1941	June 20: U.S. Army Air Forces (USAAF) created
	December 7: Japanese attack Pearl Harbor; United States enters World War II
1942	B-25 bombers attack Japan from aircraft carrier USS *Hornet*.
1943	USAAF bombers begin operations against targets in Germany
1944	June 6: USAAF takes part in invasion of Europe and subsequent operations to liberate France and other occupied countries
1945	May 8: War in Europe ends
	August 6: Atomic bomb dropped on Japanese city of Hiroshima
	August 9: Atomic bomb dropped on Japanese city of Nagasaki
	August 14: Japan surrenders
1947	September: U.S. Air Force (USAF) created as separate service
1948	USAF participates in Berlin Airlift
1950–1953	U.S. forces participate in Korean War
1964–1975	U.S. forces participate in Vietnam War
1990	USAF deploys to Iraq as part of Persian Gulf War
1991–2003	USAF aircraft patrol skies over Iraq
1995	USAF takes part in air strikes to bring peace settlement in civil war in Yugoslavia
1999	USAF leads attacks against Serbian forces in Kosovo
2001	USAF takes part in efforts to combat terrorism after September 11 attacks
2003	USAF takes part in war to remove Saddam Hussein from power in Iraq

Glossary

armament:	weapons
artillery:	weapons for discharging missiles
bloc:	a combination of persons, groups, or nations forming a unit with a common interest or purpose
communist:	someone who believes in a system in which goods are owned in common and are available to all as needed
coalition:	a temporary alliance of states or forces formed to carry out a combined action
court-martial:	a court consisting of commissioned officers and in some instances enlisted personnel for the trial of members of the armed forces or others within its jurisdiction
deterrent:	serving to turn aside, discourage, or prevent from acting
dictator:	a person who has absolute power and often rules oppressively
fuselage:	the central body portion of an aircraft designed to accommodate the crew and the passengers or cargo
guerrilla:	a person who engages in irregular warfare especially as a member of an independent unit carrying out harassment and acts of sabotage
hijack:	to commandeer (a flying airplane) especially by coercing the pilot at gunpoint
pylon:	a rigid structure on the outside of an aircraft for supporting something (as an engine or missile)
regime:	a government in power
satellite:	a manufactured object or vehicle intended to orbit the Earth, the Moon, or another celestial body
siding:	a short railroad track connected with the main track

Further Information

Books:

Alagna, Magdalena. *Life Inside the Air Force Academy*. New York: Children's Press, 2002.

Hasday, Judy L. *The Tuskegee Airmen*. Philadelphia: Chelsea House Publications, 2003.

Hopkins, Ellen and Richard Bartlett. *United States Air Force*. Chicago: Heinemann Library, 2003.

Kennedy, Robert C. *Life as an Air Force Fighter Pilot*. New York: Children's Press, 2000.

McNab, Chris. *Protecting the Nation with the U.S. Air Force*. Philadelphia: Mason Crest Publishers, 2003.

Web sites:

America's Air Force

www.af.mil/

This is the link for the USAF web site.

Air Force

www.airforce.com/index_fr.htm

This link provides information on joining the Air Force.

United States Air Force Academy

www.usafa.af.mil/

This is the web site for the United States Air Force Academy

Air Force Basic Military Training

www.lackland.af.mil/737web/

This site provides links and information on what types of training cadets go through.

Index

Page numbers in **bold** indicate photographs or illustrations

John F. Kennedy

History Maker Bios

Jane Sutcliffe

⌐ LERNER PUBLICATIONS COMPANY • MINNEAPOLIS

For Rose G. McCormick, who first taught me about John F. Kennedy.

Illustrations by Tim Parlin

Text copyright © 2005 by Jane Sutcliffe
Illustrations copyright © 2005 by Lerner Publications Company

Lerner Publications Company
A division of Lerner Publishing Group
241 First Avenue North
Minneapolis, MN 55401 U.S.A.

Website address: www.lernerbooks.com

Library of Congress Cataloging-in-Publication Data

Sutcliffe, Jane.
    John F. Kennedy / by Jane Sutcliffe.
       p.   cm. — (History maker bios)
    Includes bibliographical references (p.   ) and index.
    ISBN: 0–8225–1546–6 (lib. bdg. : alk. paper)
    1. Kennedy, John F. (John Fitzgerald), 1917–1963—Juvenile literature.
    2. Presidents—United States—Biography—Juvenile literature. I. Title.
    II. Series.
    E842.Z9S88 2005
    973.922'092—dc22   2004000554

Manufactured in the United States of America
1 2 3 4 5 6 – JR – 10 09 08 07 06 05

Table of Contents

INTRODUCTION

John F. Kennedy was the thirty-fifth president of the United States. Not everyone thought he would make a good president. Some people thought he was too young. Others said his religion was a problem.

President Kennedy worked hard to prove those people wrong. He led the United States during a dangerous time. He won the respect of the world. Then suddenly he was gone. His death shocked and saddened people everywhere.

This is his story.

1 A "MUCKER" GROWS UP

John F. Kennedy was not supposed to grow up to be president. His brother Joe was. At least that's what their father decided. And when Joseph Kennedy Sr. decided something, that was that.

John was born on May 29, 1917, in Brookline, Massachusetts. His father was a wealthy businessman. His mother was the daughter of the mayor of Boston.

John was named after his grandfather, John Fitzgerald. But everyone called him Jack. Jack was the second of nine Kennedy children. Joe was the first. All the Kennedy children liked sports and games. They raced sailboats and played rough games of touch football. They always played to win. "We don't want any losers around here," their father said. "In this family, we want winners."

The Kennedy family in 1932 (LEFT TO RIGHT): Bobby, Jack, Eunice, Jean, Mr. and Mrs. Kennedy, Patricia, Kathleen, Joe Jr., and Rosemary. Brother Teddy came along later.

Sometimes Jack couldn't play. He was sick much of the time. He had high fevers. His back hurt. His stomach bothered him.

Being sick so much made Jack skinny. Still, he was a handsome boy. He had blue eyes and thick sandy hair. When he laughed, his wide smile seemed to take up his whole face.

A TIE RACE

Jack and his brother Joe were always daring each other. Once they had a race around the block on their bikes. They set out in opposite directions. At the finish, they sped toward each other head-on. Neither would slow down or turn! The race ended in a bloody crash.

Jack needed twenty-eight stitches.

Jack (RIGHT) poses
with a few of his
fellow muckers.

When he was
fourteen, Jack went
away to high school. Joe
was already there. The
school had a lot of rules. Rules
didn't bother Joe at all. He did well at school.
But Jack was another story. He hated rules.
He was always late to class. His room was a
mess. And his grades were terrible.

The principal had a name for students like
Jack. He called them "muckers." Jack didn't
mind being called a mucker at all. In fact, he
and his friends formed the Muckers Club.
Soon there were over a dozen members.

Mostly, the boys just met in Jack's room and listened to music. But once a rumor went around the school. The Muckers were going to smuggle a pile of horse manure into a school dance. They were going to plop it right onto the dance floor!

The principal heard the rumor. That was the end of the Muckers Club. The principal called Jack's father to the school. Mr. Kennedy wasn't happy that his son was in trouble. But he was rather proud of Jack too. He saw that Jack had been a leader to the other boys.

Jack studied political science at Harvard. He also played football and competed on the swim team.

Jack (RIGHT) and Joe Jr. (LEFT) arrived in England with their father (CENTER) in the summer of 1938.

After he graduated from high school, Jack became a student at Harvard University. Then Jack's father got an important job in England. Jack took time off from Harvard to join his family there.

In 1939, Europe was headed for war. Jack traveled all over Europe. He wanted to see for himself what was going on. When he returned to Harvard, he wrote a long paper about what he had seen. Jack's professors liked his ideas. The paper helped Jack graduate from Harvard with honors.

Jack's father thought the paper would make a good book. He had friends who helped make it happen. In 1940, *Why England Slept* was published. Jack's book was a big hit.

By 1941, Jack was twenty-four. He was a Harvard graduate. He was a best-selling author and the son of a very wealthy man. Jack could have done just about anything. He decided to join the U.S. Navy. World War II was already being fought in Europe. Jack knew that soon the United States would have to join in too. He wanted to help his country when that happened.

2 PT-109

Bombs! Jack heard the word on the radio. Japanese planes had bombed the U.S. naval base at Pearl Harbor, Hawaii. The United States was at war.

Jack was sent to the Solomon Islands, in the Pacific Ocean. He took command of a small, flimsy wooden boat called a PT boat. The PT stood for "patrol torpedo." Jack's boat was *PT-109*.

The little boats patrolled the waters at night. The crew looked for enemy ships. Then they torpedoed and sank them. That was the way it was supposed to work, anyway. On many nights, Jack and his crew saw no enemy ships at all.

In the early morning of August 2, 1943, *PT-109* was on patrol as usual. There was no moon. It was so dark the crew could barely see each other, let alone a passing ship.

Jack (FAR RIGHT) poses with his crew aboard PT-109.

Jack's crew was constantly on the lookout for Japanese destroyers such as this one. The crew's job was to fire on the enemy ships and sink them.

Out of the blackness, an enemy destroyer appeared! The ship ran straight into the side of *PT-109*. With a roar, the boat's gas tanks exploded. The ship continued through the fireball, nearly cutting the PT boat in half.

Two of Jack's men were killed in the crash. The rest had to swim for an island, three miles away. One of the men was badly burned. He couldn't make the swim. Jack took the strap from the man's life jacket and put it between his teeth. Then he began swimming, towing the man along with him.

When they got to the island, the men were exhausted. Jack was exhausted too. Even so, he swam back out to look for a rescue ship that night. He saw nothing.

For the next three days, Jack swam from island to island looking for help. At last, he met two natives. The natives agreed to carry a message for Jack. Of course, Jack didn't have any paper. So he used a knife to carve his message on a coconut.

Jack's unusual message worked. Six days after the crash, the crew was rescued. Jack was awarded the Navy and Marine Corps Medal for his bravery, but he hated being called a hero. He said, "The real heroes are not the men who return, but those who stay out there . . . two of my men included."

The Coconut in the White House

Jack held on to his lucky coconut shell. When he became president, it sat on his desk in the White House.

Captain F. L. Conklin
presents the Navy and Marine
Corps Medal to Jack in 1944.

Jack's health
had always been bad.
After the shipwreck, it got worse. He
was skinnier than ever. His back hurt so
badly that he needed a cane to walk. The
navy sent him home. In June 1944, Jack
had surgery on his back. Then he went to
his family's home to rest.

He was there when the Kennedys
received terrible news. Jack's brother Joe
had been killed in the war.

Everyone, especially Jack's father, had
expected Joe to become a famous politician.
Now Joe was gone. Mr. Kennedy began to
focus on Jack instead. And Jack began to
think about a life in politics.

3 THE CAMPAIGN TRAIL

In 1946, Massachusetts needed a new representative in the U.S. Congress. Jack's father wanted him to run for the office. Jack liked the idea too. There was only one problem. None of the voters knew who Jack was. So Jack's family went to work.

Jack's father used his money to buy advertising. Jack's mother and sisters held tea parties to introduce Jack to the voters.

Jack worked hardest of all. He went to factories, fire stations, and pool halls to meet voters. He gave speeches—hundreds of them. People liked his relaxed, easy way of speaking.

His father was surprised. He saw that Jack had a natural gift for politics.

When Jack first started running for office in 1946, he was a little shy. But he kept giving speeches. Soon it was clear that he had a passion for politics.

Jack won the election easily. The voters must have liked Representative Kennedy. They reelected him twice. In 1952, he ran for the U.S. Senate. When he won that election too, he became Senator Kennedy.

One night at a dinner party, Jack met Jacqueline Bouvier. "Jackie" was young, smart, and elegant. Jack had dated many pretty women. But he had never met anyone like Jackie. Jack and Jackie dated for almost one year. On September 12, 1953, they were married.

Jackie was beautiful and smart. She had gone to school in Paris and spoke four languages.

Profiles in Courage quickly became a best-seller. Jack often signed copies of the book for his fans.

The Kennedys had not been married long when Jack needed another operation on his back. This one went badly. Jack took months to recover. He used his time to write another book. The book told the stories of eight brave Americans, including John Quincy Adams and Sam Houston. Jack called it *Profiles in Courage.*

Jack and Jackie's first child, Caroline, was born in 1957. Caroline was a delight to her proud parents. They spent as much time with her as they could.

The book won an important award, the Pulitzer Prize. The book also earned Jack a lot of attention. In 1956, Jack was nearly picked as a candidate for vice president. He lost the vote. But he saw that with hard work, he could go even further. In January 1960, Jack announced that he would run for president of the United States.

Jack knew that he was not exactly a shoo-in for president. One problem was his age. Jack was forty-three. Some people thought that was too young. But many voters liked the idea of a young president. They saw that Jack was practically bursting with energy. He promised to "get the country moving."

Jack ran for president in 1960. Whenever he gave a speech, large crowds came to hear him.

A Secret

When Jack was thirty, doctors were finally able to tell him why he was sick so much. He had an illness called Addison's disease. Jack had to take medicine for the rest of his life. No one outside his family knew this, though. Jack and his family kept his illness a secret.

Jack's religion was another problem. He was Catholic. The leader of the Roman Catholic Church is the pope, who lives in Rome. The pope is in charge of Catholics all over the world. But some people thought that the pope shouldn't tell a president of the United States what to do. There had never been a Catholic president before. These people wanted to keep it that way.

Jack went on TV. He spoke about his religion. He stood up for his right to be president. After all, "nobody asked me if I was Catholic when I joined the United States Navy," he said.

At last, Jack was named the Democratic Party's choice for president. The Republican Party chose Richard Nixon. Jack would have to beat Nixon to become president.

Jack asked Nixon to take part in a debate. The two would discuss important issues face-to-face. The debate was the first ever on TV. Millions of people watched. Most of them thought that Nixon looked nervous. There were little beads of sweat on his upper lip. Jack, on the other hand, looked calm. He seemed sure of his answers. That's how a president should look, viewers said.

This family watches a debate between Jack Kennedy and Richard Nixon. Most people thought Jack looked good on TV.

On November 8, 1960, Americans voted. It was very close. But when all the votes were counted, Jack had made history. He was the youngest person—and the first Roman Catholic—ever elected president of the United States.

A PRESIDENT'S JOB

Jack and Jackie moved into the White House with their two children. Caroline was three years old. Her little brother, John Jr., was just a baby.

Right away, Jack started a program called the Peace Corps. Peace Corps volunteers went to poor countries. They taught school. And they taught people how to build roads and plant crops.

Peace Corps volunteers live in villages with the people they are trying to help. They learn the people's language and customs.

Soon thousands of Peace Corps volunteers were making friends for the United States around the world.

Sometimes Jack had to deal with countries that did not like the United States at all. The most powerful of these countries was the Soviet Union. The two countries were not at war. But they were not exactly at peace either. People called it a "Cold War." Jack had to make sure that the Cold War did not turn into a real war.

One morning, an assistant showed Jack some photographs. The pictures showed that the Soviet Union was putting missiles on the island of Cuba. Cuba was only ninety miles away from the United States. Jack knew that this was big trouble. A nuclear missile fired from Cuba could reach a U.S. city in minutes.

NUCLEAR WARHEAD BUNKER
UNDER CONSTRUCTION
SAN CRISTOBAL SITE 1

PREFABRICATION MATERIALS

A spy plane took this photo of a missile site the Soviet Union was building in Cuba.

Jack's advisers helped him decide what to do about the missiles in Cuba.

The missiles had to be taken away, Jack knew. But how could he make that happen? His advisers wanted him to send planes to attack Cuba. Destroy the missiles, they said. Of course, any Soviets working on the missiles would be killed. That was sure to start a nuclear war with the Soviet Union. A war like that had never been fought before. Half the people in the United States could die!

Instead, Jack decided to "quarantine" Cuba. U.S. Navy ships would surround the island and make a blockade. They would stop Soviet ships from reaching Cuba. The ships would not deliver more missiles.

Jack hoped that the blockade would prevent a deadly war. But no one was quite sure what the Soviets would do. They might become so angry that they would fire their missiles anyway. The blockade might start a war after all!

On October 24, 1962, the blockade began. Over 170 U.S. ships stood ready around Cuba. Soviet ships steamed toward them. What would happen when the two sides met? All Jack could do was wait.

"WE CHOOSE TO GO TO THE MOON"

Soon after Jack became president, the Soviets launched the first human in space. Jack didn't like coming in second to the Soviets. He made a decision. He promised that the United States would be first to land an astronaut on the Moon. The United States kept Jack's promise. On July 20, 1969, Neil Armstrong became the first person to walk on the Moon.

Before the missile crisis, Jack met with the leader of the Soviet Union. The two saw eye to eye on very little.

Suddenly, word came. The Soviet ships had stopped! They were not trying to cross the quarantine line. They were turning around. The blockade had worked!

Four days later, the Soviets agreed to remove the missiles from Cuba. Jack's gamble had paid off. The crisis was over.

Sometimes danger didn't come from other countries. Sometimes it came from the American people themselves.

In the South, black Americans were asking for more rights. They held marches in the streets. Some people didn't want black Americans to have the same rights that white Americans had. There were riots. Police dogs attacked the marchers. High-pressure hoses knocked them off their feet. Angry crowds insulted them.

Three civil rights protesters are sprayed with a high-pressure fire hose. Its spray is strong enough to tear the bark from trees.

In June 1963, two black students tried to enroll at the University of Alabama. The school had never had a black student before. The governor of Alabama himself tried to stop the students. He stood in the doorway of the school and would not let them pass. It was an ugly moment. Jack had to send soldiers to end the standoff. At last, the students were admitted.

Governor George Wallace blocks a doorway at the University of Alabama.

Jack told the American people that discrimination was wrong. But not everyone agreed with him.

That night, Jack spoke to the country on TV. He spoke plainly. He said that treating people differently because of the color of their skin was simply wrong. Doing so had no place in American law. It had no place in American life.

He told people that he was asking for new laws to be passed. The laws would make sure that all Americans—white or black—would be treated the same. But it was not enough to change the law, he said. He challenged the American people to change their minds. He challenged them to change their lives.

Martin Luther King Jr. spoke to more than 250,000 people during the March on Washington.

Two months after Jack's speech, there was another march for equality. This one was in Washington, D.C. Thousands of people gathered around the Lincoln Memorial. They cheered as they listened to speeches by black leaders. One of the speakers at the march was Martin Luther King Jr. He stirred everyone who heard him with his "I Have a Dream" speech. There were no riots—not even a fistfight. Everything was peaceful.

After the march, Jack invited the leaders to the White House. He shook their hands. When he shook King's hand, Jack said, "I have a dream." It was Jack's way of saying that he had been moved by King's speech too. He told the leaders how happy he was with the march. "You made the difference," one told him. "You gave us your blessings."

Civil rights leaders meet with Jack in the White House. King is third from the left.

5 DALLAS

Not everyone was happy with the job that Jack was doing. Some were angry at what he had done for black Americans. Others wanted him to be tougher on the Soviet Union.

A new election was coming up. Jack was determined to win. That meant he would have to convince the voters he was doing a good job.

Jack decided to start his election campaign in the South. On November 22, 1963, he and Jackie went to Dallas, Texas.

The crowd that greeted Jack's plane was anything but unhappy. People were jumping up and down in excitement. They screamed and cheered as if he were a rock star. Jack called it a "real Texas welcome."

Jack and Jackie receive a warm welcome in Dallas. Jackie carries a bouquet of red roses given to her upon her arrival.

Jackie greets an enthusiastic crowd in Dallas.

Jack and Jackie shook hands with some of the crowd. Then they stepped into an open car for the ride through Dallas. The governor of Texas and his wife joined them.

The streets of Dallas were lined with people—250,000 of them. They jostled each other to get glimpses of Jack and Jackie. They leaned out of windows for a better view. The roar of their cheers drowned out the sound of the motorcycles riding alongside Jack's car.

Jack and Jackie ride through the streets of Dallas.

Crack!

Suddenly, a sharp noise echoed through the streets. A car backfiring, thought some people. Firecrackers, thought others.

But they were wrong. The sound was a gunshot.

A bullet streaked over the heads of the crowd. It hit Jack. A moment later, another bullet followed. This one also struck him. Jack slumped to the side of his seat in the car.

The president had been shot! The car roared forward. It raced to the hospital. But it was too late. A short time later, the official word came. At age forty-six, John F. Kennedy was dead.

Radio and TV announcers told people what had happened. The nation was stunned by the horrible news. All over the country, people stopped what they were doing. For the rest of their lives, they would remember where they had been at that moment.

People all over the world mourned the death of Jack Kennedy.

HISTORY ON WHEELS

The car that Jack rode in was specially made for the president of the United States. Officially, it was called X-100. After Jack died, four more presidents used the car—Lyndon B. Johnson, Richard Nixon, Gerald Ford, and Jimmy Carter. In 1977, the car went to the Henry Ford Museum. It was put on display as a piece of United States history.

John F. Kennedy had been president for only 1,036 days. In that short time, he had made the country safer. He had set the nation on a new road to equal rights for black Americans. He had encouraged Americans to aim for the Moon and the stars. He had opened a door to a new future for the American people. But they would have to meet the future without him. John F. Kennedy was gone.

TIMELINE

JOHN F. KENNEDY WAS BORN ON MAY 29, 1917.

In the year . . .

1935   John F. Kennedy graduated from high school.

1940   he graduated from Harvard in June.
his book *Why England Slept* was published in August.   Age 23

1941   he joined the U.S. Navy in October.
the United States entered World War II on December 8.

1943   *PT-109* was sunk on August 2.

1946   Jack was first elected to the U.S. House of Representatives.   Age 29

1952   he was first elected to the U.S. Senate.

1953   he married Jacqueline Bouvier on September 12.

1956   his book *Profiles in Courage* was published.

1960   he was elected president of the United States.   Age 43

1961   he created the Peace Corps.

1962   he announced a quarantine to end the Soviet shipment of missiles to Cuba.

1963   he announced new laws to give equal rights to black Americans in June.   Age 46
he was killed in Dallas, Texas, on November 22.
he was awarded the Presidential Medal of Freedom by President Johnson in December.

WHO KILLED THE PRESIDENT?

L ee Harvey Oswald was arrested for killing President Kennedy. Two days later, he too was shot and killed. There was no trial. So there was no way to judge what had happened on November 22, 1963. Some people wondered whether or not Oswald really was the killer.

Over the years, people have pointed fingers at all sorts of suspects. Some said a group of criminals killed Kennedy. Others said it was spies from some foreign country. Some even said it was agents from the U.S. government itself.

No one has ever found anything to prove these stories. All the evidence points to Oswald. Still, some people continue to ask: Who really killed John F. Kennedy?

Lee Harvey Oswald (RIGHT) was shot as he was being moved to a different prison on November 24, 1963.

FURTHER READING

Anderson, Catherine Corley. *Jacqueline Kennedy Onassis: Woman of Courage.* **Minneapolis: Lerner Publications Company, 1995.** This biography tells the life story of the former First Lady.

Chrisp, Peter. *The Cuban Missile Crisis.* **Milwaukee, WI: World Almanac, 2002.** A good overview of the Cuban Missile Crisis.

Cooper, Ilene. *Jack: The Early Years of John F. Kennedy.* **New York: Dutton Books, 2003.** An account of Jack's childhood, accompanied by black-and-white photos.

Finlayson, Reggie. *We Shall Overcome: The History of the American Civil Rights Movement.* **Minneapolis: Lerner Publications Company, 2003.** A vivid history of the civil rights movement in the United States.

Hampton, Wilborn. *Kennedy Assassinated!: The World Mourns: A Reporter's Story.* **Cambridge, MA: Candlewick Press, 1997.** A behind-the-scenes look at the day Kennedy was assassinated.

Heiligman, Deborah. *High Hopes: A Photobiography of John F. Kennedy.* **Washington, DC: National Geographic, 2003.** A beautifully illustrated overview of Jack and his family.

Levine, Ellen. *Freedom's Children: Young Civil Rights Activists Tell Their Own Stories.* **Madison, WI: Turtleback Books, 2001.** Inspiring stories of children and teenagers who contributed to the civil rights movement.

WEBSITES

The White House: John Kennedy
<http://www.whitehouse.gov/history/presdents/jk35html>
Visitors to this website can learn about Jack's life.

The Peace Corps
<www.peacecorps.gov> Learn all about the Peace Corps at
this informative website, including where corps volunteers
work and what they do.

SELECT BIBLIOGRAPHY

Ballard, Robert D. "The Search for PT-109." *National
Geographic*, December 2002, 78–87.

Bishop, Jim. *The Day Kennedy Was Shot*. New York: Funk
& Wagnalls, 1968.

Dallek, Robert. "The Medical Ordeals of JFK." *Atlantic
Monthly*, December 2002, 49–61.

Hamilton, Nigel. *JFK: Reckless Youth*. New York: Random
House, 1992.

Kennedy, John F. *The Greatest Speeches of President John F.
Kennedy*. Bellingham, WA: Titan Publishing, 2001.

Kenney, Charles. *John F. Kennedy: The Presidential
Portfolio: History as Told through the Collection of the
John F. Kennedy Library and Museum*. New York:
PublicAffairs, 2000.

*Report of the President's Commission on the Assassination
of President Kennedy*. Washington, DC: U.S.
Government Printing Office, 1964.

INDEX

Acknowledgments

For photographs and artwork: The John F. Kennedy Library, pp. 4, 7, 9, 10, 11, 14, 17, 19, 21, 23, 29, 30, 32, 35, 37, 39, 40; © CORBIS, p 15; *The New Bedford Standard-Times,* p. 20; © Bettmann/CORBIS, pp. 22, 33, 42; National Archives, p. 25; The Peace Corps, p. 28; © Hulton|Archive by Getty Images, p. 34; © Hulton-Deutsch Collection/ CORBIS, p. 36; The Everett Collection, pp. 41, 45; Front Cover: John F. Kennedy Library; Back Cover: © David J. and Janice L. Frent Collection/CORBIS.
For quoted material: pp. 7, 16, Nigel Hamilton, *JFK: Reckless Youth* (New York: Random House, 1992); pp. 23, 24, 37, Charles Kenney, *John F. Kennedy: The Presidential Portfolio: History as Told through the Collection of the John F. Kennedy Library and Museum* (New York: PublicAffairs, 2000); p. 30, *John F. Kennedy, The Greatest Speeches of President John F. Kennedy* (Bellingham, WA: Titan Publishing, 2001); p. 37, Richard Reeves, *President Kennedy: Profile of Power* (New York: Simon & Schuster, 1993); p. 39, Jim Bishop, *The Day Kennedy Was Shot* (New York: Funk & Wagnalls, 1968).